THE BUSY-NESS PSYCHOLOGIST

ON A

DESTINATION GUIDE

Content

Introduction

Destination guide and the busy-ness psychology is yet another must read title from Atisu Delanyo, in this must read intriguing title for everyone who want to take business/ entrepreneurship seriously or probably want to find-out why is entrepreneurship/business should matter or be taken seriously. Destination guide is the inspiration while busy-ness psychology is the title message; a practical functional teachings and its applicable directly to real life situations.

ABOUT THE AUTHOR

Atisu Delanyo is an author writer and motivational speaker, he describe himself as a busy-ness psychologist simply because been busy or the act of business itself is what make us busy(and vice versa), been busy without been in business is a complete waste of time and energy, he teaches how we can convert our very own busy-ness into business, profiting from our everyday busy-ness is the best way to financial freedom in fact most successful people seems not to be busy or have most of the time which is only possible because they enjoy what they do best and convert that into their business.

BUSY-NESS AND BUSINESS

Business is an adjectives of busy i.e. to say how busy are you I'm busy-ness, however the word business has evolved been crafted into a different meaning, other than its original meaning 'busy', this has created the 'very' busy to qualify how busy one is i.e. very busy, while the word business has emerge into a more commercial/profit venture activities, nevertheless we are all 'buys-ness men and women in many ways the only difference is that some are able to build a more commercial profit venture around their busy-ness activities hence they are known business person.

You have been busy lately and always busy still nothing to show for all the busy-ness, learn to build a business around your 'busy-ness' and if your busy-ness is not profitable/commercial viable it's time to drop that busy-ness and be busy with a bankable /profitable busy-ness.

Business is not all about setting up a company or an extensive entrepreneurship venture, the act of doing profitable business start from the mind with a core motives of solving a problem, making life/things better for everyone or at least many or doing just what you like doing best, in as much as making profit is the overall objectives in the every business it shouldn't be the core, many business fail because they are too profit eccentric without creating any solution or helping anyone. The mind mine is the most expensive and resourceful mine ever there is and I always recommend everyone to keep mining their mind busy-ness.

The busy-ness of the twenty first century is all mining the mind busy-ness that is what the wealthiest people trade on the mind mine

Quick fact about the mind mine

- All discoveries start with the mind mine
- All invention was first invented in the mind
- All resource in this world are deposited in the mind
- Ideas is the most expensive resource ever there is
- The mind mine cannot be sold or bought, it cannot be copied or duplicated however it may be faked/imitated (to copy or

duplicate means the new copied or duplicated has the original features which is not possible with the mind mine ideas but when its faked/imitated it does not have the original features hence it's been regarded as innovation/creativity)

- The grave is rumored to be the richest place on earth simply because there you will find ideas never achieved
- The Value of the mind mice depends on experience and time
- The currency that the mind mine trade on is believe/hope and integrity, without believe one ideas will soon be bereaved.

- The mind busy-ness is not for smart people it's for intelligent people
- The mind busy-ness is not for those who cannot think far
- The mind busy-ness is not for doubt/confusion/comparison /argument/disbelieve or discouragement
- The mind busy-ness is all about who you are , you can't be someone else
- The mind busy-ness understands the times.

THE BUSY-NESS PSYCHOLOGY

The busy-ness psychology is the study of the mind mine that helps one to discover the potentials viability of one mind busy-ness and the mind mine.

The psychology of negotiation is yet another important fabric of the busy-ness mind, these topic deals with negotiation and striking positive good deals with the mind currency which is believe, hope and integrity, psychology check unbalances is usually very common among growing youths the usual element of psychological checks unbalances are disbelieve, doubt, confusion, argument, stress these element usually comes in different packages either in family, relationship, socio economic etc. mostly unaware to many they disarray psychological processing usually incubating the mind mine and when these happen the result is having people with so many vast potentials but only able to deliver less than 1% a situation we may term as dilute thinking.

FOUR BUSY-NESS CHOICES

A.   The choice to do things rightly even though it may not be getting result instantly

B.   The choice to do things anyhow has long as it get result

C.   The choice to do what everyone does as long as it get result

D.   The choice to stick to the wrong things even though it gets no results.

Naming the four choices;

A.   Will become the choice of integrity

B.   Will become the choice of eventuality

C.   Will become blind crowd following

D.   Pre-determined failure.

Explanations

A.   The choice of integrity, the subject integrity is much easy to define than to be practiced. In achieving success there are many element/character needed usually boldness, courage, focus, determination, respect, honesty, hard work, smartness, dedication, been inspired or motivated, been coached or to be trained, been talented or gifted all these character are much more easy to learn and practiced but there is nothing as difficult as practicing integrity itself doing what is right even when no one is watching it may not be getting result/ benefit, doing what is right even when you can easily do something smart.

In real world of business where competition is very endemic, integrity does not thrive, however the few who decide to go down on the path of integrity always become the biggest loser or winner, the path of integrity does not guarantee success that is why it's a choice so if you stick to these choice remember you may still end up losing everything. Becoming the biggest gainer with integrity is not a bed of roses it's not promised or given it's taken by force (the kingdom of heaven suffers violence and with violence it's taken by force) in winning with integrity it involves one catalyst called 'master craft'. The making of master craft is to be focus and determined to win and never giving up on the right things/integrity, a master craftsmanship understand there are many things he may let-go in order to achieve success but never giving-up, letting go is like lighting the ship during storm but not quitting the journey because of storm so you let go of certain loads in order to face the storm.

A master craft understand that not everyone will buy into his craft so he target the right market, stop wasting time on the wrong friends, relation, companies, take a bold step to swim from that little pond into the sea and ocean, master craft accept challenges and don't conform to his environment alone, master craft is a learner and keeps learning, the sad part of the master craft is that he is never the best the most gifted or talented in keep learning.

B. The choice of eventuality: they have plan but don't understand plan, they have strategy but cannot strategies, they have talent but no character, they know it all but do nothing or less, many fall in this category hence they seem to be dominating they system, from afar they are very rich, famous, sometimes called the big shot but when you move closer they are so empty and what you see from afar is just an illusion from within they are so broke and empty, discontent. Eventually they may blossom at some point or the other but their reality is that blossom soon dies/fade-out.

C.   Blind/crowd following: they end up following the choice of eventuality and their own crowd, usually Band C cycle round the same circle they eat from the same pot but what differ is that C mainly are pure followers and copycats as long as there is a crowd they follow without knowing what the crowd gathering is about or objectives they just follow without asking why and usually carried away, they usually are short sighted and demand quick benefit or reward

D.   Pre-determined failure: I don't understand this choice enough but yes some will still join the bus leading to failure. There is no problem trying to understand or study the action of a mad man but there is a big problem trying to understand or study 'madness'. It important to study the cause of a problem in other to create a solution but there is no sense studying the problem itself. Many are struck in their complication of problems because they waste time talking about the problems rather than finding out the root cause of the problem and finding solution they simply enjoy the blame game. successful people or to be successful you need to focus on nothing else but finding answers to every problems and taking responsibility what separate the successful from the failures is that one take responsibility and find answers/solution to every challenging problematic situation confronting him while the other simply enjoy the blame game and been content with complaining why or how there is not enough this and that.

DESTINATION GUIDE

We do have vision, goals and the ultimate purpose is that we arrive at a place called destiny, destiny is where one get to live an do the things one always wanted to, the process of getting there is DESTINATION and one must be guided through inspiration, coaching, teachings or motivation and one key channel is through reading (like reading the destination guide book series) arriving at ones vision goals success is destiny.

DESTINAY AND DESTINATION: The word destiny is a noun it origin id from Latin

Latin meaning destinare---destinata, which means make firm or establish

The word Destination also is a noun it origin Latin

not achieved their very robust plans sometimes unrealistic, mostly they live all their lives working for tomorrow and they never get to live for today even for one seconds.

- Live today for tomorrow: these is combining the first two way of living, the ones who live this live are usually very functionally and achiever they are good planners, thinkers and strategist. They are very honest and realistic and live well today so they can face tomorrow whiles planning fir tomorrow as well.

CHARACTER ASSINATION

Character assassination is when people judge your motives/intention wrongly or when your actions does not match your words in as much as actions speaks louder than words when the actions is too louds it may distorts the understanding of the words also the situation is not different when it's too silent, best practice will be balancing the actions and words.

In a world where action speaks louder than words, intention/motives or the state of the mind is no nonsense to many, many don't have the time to access your intention/motives or the state of the mind but are too quick to judge one's character/actions. In as much as to a very large extent character/action can be a true reflection of ones motives or intention it's not always true to concludes that one's character/actions is the true reflection of one's motives/intention, many have their character assassinating their thought, character assassination is simply a condition/Situation where one's intention/motives does not reflect their true actions/character hence they are wrongly judged.

It takes only a functionally observer (the one accessing/judging) one's character to see beyond what he sees, and also it takes a, functionally personality to always makes his intention /motives clear enough, there are so many factors that may leads to character assassination, it could be political, socio-economical, relationship or family related. It's important not to allow these factors to behold your imagination as these factors dilute /pollute everything hence creating a fake situation that tends to mimic your true personality.

When people start reacting to external factors/pressure they lose focus/concentration and self-worth, that's when the character assassination theory set in. The successful have the highest state of mental stability (focus\) they are usually seen not to be affected by any form of external factor but does it means they don't feel it or understand the situation everyone is going through? The answer is no as a matter of fact most successful people have the most difficult situation facing them but they have learned not to allow those situation to weigh them down rather they concentrate on their mind busy-ness (mind-mine) which is the most expensive mine ever there is in the world.

FACTORS LEADING TO CHARACTER ASSASINATION

- Unbalanced actions to words: Actions speaks louder than words, when one actions is too loud this means people are most likely to believe your actions than when you speak, hence in your absence or in situation when people cannot relate with your actions character/ personality they don't take your messages/words seriously or the enthusiasm as to how they will accept your words is too cold, these mostly affect people in high offices/leaders functional leader should learn to relate with his followers on and off the action parameters these may be achieved by delegations (allow others to take your place) don't wait until when you are completely incapacitated, consistency is another important factor be consistent as much as possible it foster good relationship and understanding words are powerful but without the right packaging which is "actions" it becomes so useless and helpless however note that "actions" cannot be over emphasized. Some notable actions include your posture, appearance, the use of voice, in using these notable actions be sure to understand when, why, where and mostly the timings to use them.

- Dealing with closed minded individuals; No one can go through a closed door except its first open, in the same sense closed minded individual will keep judging you wrongly except their closed mind is open. closed mindedness is a condition when an individual has a certain or reaction to a specific situation without due recourse mostly as a result of past experience for instance a boy grew-up having lot of bitter experience with women including his mother hence he grew-up believing all women are the same (note it could be vice versa) to this boy he has not experienced a good caring loving women so not matter the story or examples you may give his mind is simply shut, mostly closed minded individual are usually very difficult to deal with its best to help them experience the better and brighter side.

- Circumstantial pre-judged credentials knowing or un-knowing to you people use recent circumstances, happening or situation to judge interestingly most people do these things unconsciously, circumstantial pre-judge credential differs from closed mind such that in these case people made their judgments unconsciously and have no experience they simply based their judgment/assessment on what they have heard or seen and are likely to give a try/test but note when their first try testing becomes positive (that conforms to what they have seen or heard) then their mind becomes closed for instance a child was told not to play with fire because fire burn, when the child decide to ignore those warning and try to play with fire the fire surely burn the child severely next time his mind is completely closed towards playing with fire

- In experienced; in experience leads to character assassination in many ways but the good news is one's experience grows/develop automatically people will begins to give you better credit/judgments being experienced not even the legends or the most talented experienced simply appreciate with time

CHARACTER INTERVIEWING

Character interviewing is very common but many are unaware when or how it's taking place, character interviewing is simply the process when one's interpersonal relationship skills is noted to determine if its fit/acceptable for both parties or third parties or the socio-organization community as a whole

Most often when prospective candidate are called for a job interview they mostly make mistake to sound too intellectual, theoretical and or calculative in fact interview is simply a set-up to know the individual personally, regarding your intellectual or experience qualification they have assessed those already based on your curriculum vitae- (cv) and cover letters, interview is mostly set-up to know the individual personally (character) as a matter of fact some employee don't mind spending more resources training the right candidate with the right character with little or less experience and qualification than those with only experience and qualification. Character interviewing is one key aspect of every interview that most don't prepare for and also usually the final determinate as to whether one candidate will get the job or not, many prospective candidate end up assassinating their character in the process because their main focus is on qualities, theories or intellectual abilities forgetting their character abilities. It's very wrong and un-ethical to believe one personality or character does not matter or qualifies a person in any organization or cooperate setting, in every organization or corporate setting personality and character forms an integral part of their policies and ethical standards in as much as it may be very silent, these is because many organization want to be very diversify as much as possible I other to accommodate and work with a diverse cultural employees and customers/clients, nevertheless one thing is certain and that's is one must adjust to fit into the organization ethical standards.

FUNDAMENTALS IN UNDERSTANDING CHARACTER INTERVIEWING

- Always ask question, make research about the person/company or origination before appearing
- Present yourself as someone who can fit perfectly into their cultural/ethical standards
- Present yourself as someone who has the solution they need
- Remember experience, qualities comes last, the right places/organization are willing to invest to train or help you gather more skill experience if you got the

right character and can fit perfectly into their culture.

Never waist time on the wrong places/organization they ask for too much, expect one to be super-here or super perfect and when you make the smallest error that can be corrected they penalize you severely, they always want to prove that you are not the best practically their culture is chaotic, everyone is trying to be better the other, strive, jealousy and envy persist there

- Stop seeking benefit or rewards, seek partners/organization with the right culture that you can relate with or that you can fit into

RELEVANCE OF BEING A GOOD CUSTOMER

We are customers and salesperson in many ways, mostly being a good customer is mostly not talked about or taught, the fact is a good customer is equally a good salesperson so it takes a good customer to be a good salesperson, customer who most demand fair treatment from salesperson without they been fair to the salesperson usually are the worst sales person. been a salesperson or customer is not all about goods and services, one's character, ideas, innovation ,creativity and general personality requires selling and others buying into you, without others buying into your ideas, innovation, character and creativity one remains stagnant and will have lot of interpersonal relationship challenges.

No one want to be around people with bad interpersonal skills, so no one want to do business with bad customers even if the customer is the biggest buyer/spender, some will try to sell to do business with bad customers because of their money but sooner or later when they have enough of it or when they have other better customers to do business with they will surely walk away and that's when the bad customers. complain about un-satisfaction to a large extent bad customer complain about un-satisfaction and no matter how good a salesperson maybe they still cannot satisfy bad customers enough. No salesperson with good product want to sell to bad customers, so technically bad customers end-up buying the wrong/bad goods from the bad/worst salesperson all the time. To the salesperson who wants to take advantage of innocent/good customers always have themselves to blame because at the end they lose the good customers to the bad ones, more importantly we are all customers and salesperson in many ways good customers attract good salesperson and vice versa.

MERIT AND DEMERIT OF GOOD AND BAD CUSTOMERS

GOOD CUSTOMER/SA LESPERSON	BAD CUSTOMER/SA LESPERSON
Good customer/sales person compliment an inexperience salesperson (vice versa)	Bad customers simply complain about everything even when an inexperience salesperson is putting up his best (vice versa)
Good customer testifies about a very good product	Bad customer keeps complaining even if the product is good

	enough
Good customer stays with the good product	Bad customer keep moving on, they cannot be satisfied enough
They know what they want	They are always uncertain about their choices hence they can easily be moved by other substitutes
They can be planned/accounted for due to their loyalty	They cannot be planned/or accounted for
They know about the value and price	They don't care about value/price or

of what they are buying, and cares about quality	quality, they buy to keep an ego/status/clas s or just care about quantity

NOTE: practically the subject good or bad customer /salesperson is undefined, a good customer to one may be a bad customer to another (same applies to salesperson) It's important to understand the product/service the market/economy and the buyer practically some bad/fake product sells even much more than the original, good or bad customer as used here is only fictitious and does not literally represent good or bad. The understanding of who is a good or bad to customer/salesperson helps to target the right market make quality market research and development analysis.

EXPERIENCE THE BEST TEACHER

Nobody qualifies you because you have learnt from so many experiences, they only qualifies you base on your experience and what you have learnt from it (them).

Experience is the best teacher, and not learner! Let experience teach you and not learning from other's experiences, in order words go through your experience to learn and not learning from other's experiences.

Experience is the best safest ways to learn money cannot buy experience, experience cannot be taught that's why its experience, it cannot be transferred, inherited, modified, borrowed, copied, faked and that's why you have to experience one. In as much as learning from others experience is good to one not making bad choices/mistake one cannot live/be successful based on others experiences.

HOW TO BUILD AN EXPEREICE PORTFOLIO

1.   Plan to fail; many only plan to succeed and mostly their plan strategy fails them, and they only realize they have failed terribly, but planning to fail gives you the experience in order to better your actual plans/strategy.

2. Be early so you can hurry, and when you are late don't hurry, when you are early be hurry so you have enough time to strategize should in case something go wrong with your original plan you still have enough time to correct them and still meet-up with the required timing and when you're late there is no point to be hurry be calm to observe, this will help you to pick the pieces that may be a good recipe to make innovative/creative alternatives.

3. Think more talk less, do more. Think more to do more and when you cannot think more just keep doing more as much as possible avoid too much talking.

4.	Be practical oriented, avoid unnecessary analysis, information or theories instead focus on how to apply the little you have learnt/know.

5.	Be definitive and consistent, many times some goals/plans may lack clear definition and understanding to many, that's why you've to be very definitive and be consistent enough when consistency anchor cannot holds any longer be persistent, in order to be definitive these may require breaking the goals/plans into smaller units these is where creativity and innovation comes to play thereby appealing to a wider demography's.

6. Time itself is undefined (learn more about time in understanding 30chapters of time) so time cannot measure experience accurately, people will value your experience not because of your age or how long but by the rich deliverables you've achieved or can do with your experience.

SOME ILLOGICAL POPULAR SAYINGS

1. People address you the way you dress: it's obvious that those who address you the way you dress are addressing your dress and not "you" they are admiring your dress! The saying people address you the way you dress does not have sound moral values, they only admire or address the dress and not the person wearing the dress it's like pouring water into a basket. Let people address you for

who you are not what you have become, when all you have is the company of folks who only come together to celebrate your success (dresses) you will soon wake-up someday to realize that those friends companies are no more (they have gone to celebrate elsewhere) instead celebrates with the company of those who stood by you when the success (dresses) were not there.

Have you ever wonder, what is the relationship between "dressings" and "addresses" why should addresses proportionate dressing of what benefit/importance is dressing to addresses? Again dressing and addresses should not be confused with personal grooming/branding or hygiene, personal grooming/branding or hygiene goes beyond dressing, your personal grooming is who you are. Your personality and more importantly modesty is at the center of these but dressing is your packaging and not you.

2. Money talks: money does not have mouth and money cannot talk. Those who are carried away by the saying "money talks" are the same people who are carried away

with lust and vanity of life, the fact is having or not having money does not make or change anything but the positive impact of what is done/achieved with money is what make the difference. Furthermore there are many in the world today all they have is money to show-off but they make no impact or live any legacy behind.

3. First impression count: first impression does not matter a lasting impression counts, in many cases all what people have is first impression to show and then nothing more, others waist too much effort on first impression

alone that afterwards they fade quickly away like flowers some never start at all because they have not gotten the first impression to show, Leave a lasting impression because it last forever.

4.   The rich get richer while the poor get poorer: getting richer or poorer is a matter of choice and state of the mind, with the right thinking and the right attitude towards work and wealth creation anyone can be rich

5.   Your colleagues don't have two or ten heads: Many ends up competing with their follows without any clear

purpose also end-up chasing the dust because they have not discovered their true self-worth. A story was told in the bible about a master who was about to set-out in a journey he called out all his servant and gave them talent five three and one respectively, the servant who received the least went to bury his one talent because he expected to have received more. The fact is who all have different characteristics and abilities it's very important to discover your unique abilities and qualities this is the key to be a better you and be satisfied, usually those who thinks their mate, colleagues or friends cannot be better or cannot achieved more than they have only becomes frustrated and miserable with themselves.

NOTE: This is not to undermine the veracity of these saying actually these saying are true and factual to many enough, but the motives and understanding to these saying has become polluted/corrupted hence creating a dismay for analytical thinker, while confusing many who then abuse these sayings. The objectives of this content are to positively shape thinking philosophies and our thinking philosophies should be positive

oriented and should not contradict
the law.